MONTHLY BANK RECONCILIATION STATEMENT LOG

MONTHLY BANK RECONCILIATION STATEMENT

SUMMARY

Period:

Previous Balance:

Ending Balance:

Transaction Date	Description	Debit (withdrawals)	Credit (Deposits)	Balance
Total Transactions				

MONTHLY BANK RECONCILIATION STATEMENT

SUMMARY

Period:

Previous Balance:

Ending Balance:

Transaction Date	Description	Debit (withdrawals)	Credit (Deposits)	Balance
Total Transactions				

MONTHLY BANK RECONCILIATION STATEMENT

SUMMARY

Period:

Previous Balance:

Ending Balance:

Transaction Date	Description	Debit (withdrawals)	Credit (Deposits)	Balance
Total Transactions				

MONTHLY BANK RECONCILIATION STATEMENT

SUMMARY

Period:

Previous Balance:

Ending Balance:

Transaction Date	Description	Debit (withdrawals)	Credit (Deposits)	Balance
Total Transactions				

MONTHLY BANK RECONCILIATION STATEMENT

SUMMARY

Period:

Previous Balance:

Ending Balance:

Transaction Date	Description	Debit (withdrawals)	Credit (Deposits)	Balance
Total Transactions				

MONTHLY BANK RECONCILIATION STATEMENT

SUMMARY

Period:

Previous Balance:

Ending Balance:

Transaction Date	Description	Debit (withdrawals)	Credit (Deposits)	Balance
Total Transactions				

MONTHLY BANK RECONCILIATION STATEMENT

SUMMARY

Period:

Previous Balance:

Ending Balance:

Transaction Date	Description	Debit (withdrawals)	Credit (Deposits)	Balance
Total Transactions				

MONTHLY BANK RECONCILIATION STATEMENT

SUMMARY

Period:

Previous Balance:

Ending Balance:

Transaction Date	Description	Debit (withdrawals)	Credit (Deposits)	Balance
Total Transactions				

MONTHLY BANK RECONCILIATION STATEMENT

SUMMARY

Period:

Previous Balance:

Ending Balance:

Transaction Date	Description	Debit (withdrawals)	Credit (Deposits)	Balance
Total Transactions				

MONTHLY BANK RECONCILIATION STATEMENT

SUMMARY

Period:

Previous Balance:

Ending Balance:

Transaction Date	Description	Debit (withdrawals)	Credit (Deposits)	Balance
Total Transactions				

MONTHLY BANK RECONCILIATION STATEMENT

SUMMARY

Period:

Previous Balance:

Ending Balance:

Transaction Date	Description	Debit (withdrawals)	Credit (Deposits)	Balance
Total Transactions				

MONTHLY BANK RECONCILIATION STATEMENT

SUMMARY

Period:

Previous Balance:

Ending Balance:

Transaction Date	Description	Debit (withdrawals)	Credit (Deposits)	Balance
Total Transactions				

MONTHLY BANK RECONCILIATION STATEMENT

SUMMARY

Period:

Previous Balance:

Ending Balance:

Transaction Date	Description	Debit (withdrawals)	Credit (Deposits)	Balance
Total Transactions				

MONTHLY BANK RECONCILIATION STATEMENT

SUMMARY

Period:

Previous Balance:

Ending Balance:

Transaction Date	Description	Debit (withdrawals)	Credit (Deposits)	Balance
Total Transactions				

MONTHLY BANK RECONCILIATION STATEMENT

SUMMARY

Period:

Previous Balance:

Ending Balance:

Transaction Date	Description	Debit (withdrawals)	Credit (Deposits)	Balance
Total Transactions				

MONTHLY BANK RECONCILIATION STATEMENT

SUMMARY

Period:

Previous Balance:

Ending Balance:

Transaction Date	Description	Debit (withdrawals)	Credit (Deposits)	Balance
Total Transactions				

MONTHLY BANK RECONCILIATION STATEMENT

SUMMARY

Period:

Previous Balance:

Ending Balance:

Transaction Date	Description	Debit (withdrawals)	Credit (Deposits)	Balance
Total Transactions				

MONTHLY BANK RECONCILIATION STATEMENT

SUMMARY

Period:

Previous Balance:

Ending Balance:

Transaction Date	Description	Debit (withdrawals)	Credit (Deposits)	Balance
Total Transactions				

MONTHLY BANK RECONCILIATION STATEMENT

SUMMARY

Period:

Previous Balance:

Ending Balance:

Transaction Date	Description	Debit (withdrawals)	Credit (Deposits)	Balance
Total Transactions				

MONTHLY BANK RECONCILIATION STATEMENT

SUMMARY

Period:

Previous Balance:

Ending Balance:

Transaction Date	Description	Debit (withdrawals)	Credit (Deposits)	Balance
Total Transactions				

MONTHLY BANK RECONCILIATION STATEMENT

SUMMARY

Period:

Previous Balance:

Ending Balance:

Transaction Date	Description	Debit (withdrawals)	Credit (Deposits)	Balance
Total Transactions				

MONTHLY BANK RECONCILIATION STATEMENT

SUMMARY

Period:

Previous Balance:

Ending Balance:

Transaction Date	Description	Debit (withdrawals)	Credit (Deposits)	Balance
Total Transactions				

MONTHLY BANK RECONCILIATION STATEMENT

SUMMARY

Period:

Previous Balance:

Ending Balance:

Transaction Date	Description	Debit (withdrawals)	Credit (Deposits)	Balance
Total Transactions				

MONTHLY BANK RECONCILIATION STATEMENT

SUMMARY

Period:

Previous Balance:

Ending Balance:

Transaction Date	Description	Debit (withdrawals)	Credit (Deposits)	Balance
Total Transactions				

MONTHLY BANK RECONCILIATION STATEMENT

SUMMARY

Period:

Previous Balance:

Ending Balance:

Transaction Date	Description	Debit (withdrawals)	Credit (Deposits)	Balance
Total Transactions				

MONTHLY BANK RECONCILIATION STATEMENT

SUMMARY

Period:

Previous Balance:

Ending Balance:

Transaction Date	Description	Debit (withdrawals)	Credit (Deposits)	Balance
Total Transactions				

MONTHLY BANK RECONCILIATION STATEMENT

SUMMARY

Period:

Previous Balance:

Ending Balance:

Transaction Date	Description	Debit (withdrawals)	Credit (Deposits)	Balance
Total Transactions				

MONTHLY BANK RECONCILIATION STATEMENT

SUMMARY

Period:

Previous Balance:

Ending Balance:

Transaction Date	Description	Debit (withdrawals)	Credit (Deposits)	Balance
Total Transactions				

MONTHLY BANK RECONCILIATION STATEMENT

SUMMARY

Period:

Previous Balance:

Ending Balance:

Transaction Date	Description	Debit (withdrawals)	Credit (Deposits)	Balance
Total Transactions				

MONTHLY BANK RECONCILIATION STATEMENT

SUMMARY

Period:

Previous Balance:

Ending Balance:

Transaction Date	Description	Debit (withdrawals)	Credit (Deposits)	Balance
Total Transactions				

MONTHLY BANK RECONCILIATION STATEMENT

SUMMARY

Period:

Previous Balance:

Ending Balance:

Transaction Date	Description	Debit (withdrawals)	Credit (Deposits)	Balance
Total Transactions				

MONTHLY BANK RECONCILIATION STATEMENT

SUMMARY

Period:

Previous Balance:

Ending Balance:

Transaction Date	Description	Debit (withdrawals)	Credit (Deposits)	Balance
Total Transactions				

MONTHLY BANK RECONCILIATION STATEMENT

SUMMARY

Period:

Previous Balance:

Ending Balance:

Transaction Date	Description	Debit (withdrawals)	Credit (Deposits)	Balance
Total Transactions				

MONTHLY BANK RECONCILIATION STATEMENT

SUMMARY

Period:

Previous Balance:

Ending Balance:

Transaction Date	Description	Debit (withdrawals)	Credit (Deposits)	Balance
Total Transactions				

MONTHLY BANK RECONCILIATION STATEMENT

SUMMARY

Period:

Previous Balance:

Ending Balance:

Transaction Date	Description	Debit (withdrawals)	Credit (Deposits)	Balance
Total Transactions				

MONTHLY BANK RECONCILIATION STATEMENT

SUMMARY

Period:

Previous Balance:

Ending Balance:

Transaction Date	Description	Debit (withdrawals)	Credit (Deposits)	Balance
Total Transactions				

MONTHLY BANK RECONCILIATION STATEMENT

SUMMARY

Period:

Previous Balance:

Ending Balance:

Transaction Date	Description	Debit (withdrawals)	Credit (Deposits)	Balance
Total Transactions				

MONTHLY BANK RECONCILIATION STATEMENT

SUMMARY

Period:

Previous Balance:

Ending Balance:

Transaction Date	Description	Debit (withdrawals)	Credit (Deposits)	Balance
Total Transactions				

MONTHLY BANK RECONCILIATION STATEMENT

SUMMARY

Period:

Previous Balance:

Ending Balance:

Transaction Date	Description	Debit (withdrawals)	Credit (Deposits)	Balance
Total Transactions				

MONTHLY BANK RECONCILIATION STATEMENT

SUMMARY

Period:

Previous Balance:

Ending Balance:

Transaction Date	Description	Debit (withdrawals)	Credit (Deposits)	Balance
Total Transactions				

MONTHLY BANK RECONCILIATION STATEMENT

SUMMARY

Period:

Previous Balance:

Ending Balance:

Transaction Date	Description	Debit (withdrawals)	Credit (Deposits)	Balance
Total Transactions				

MONTHLY BANK RECONCILIATION STATEMENT

SUMMARY

Period:

Previous Balance:

Ending Balance:

Transaction Date	Description	Debit (withdrawals)	Credit (Deposits)	Balance
Total Transactions				

MONTHLY BANK RECONCILIATION STATEMENT

SUMMARY

Period:

Previous Balance:

Ending Balance:

Transaction Date	Description	Debit (withdrawals)	Credit (Deposits)	Balance
Total Transactions				

MONTHLY BANK RECONCILIATION STATEMENT

SUMMARY

Period:

Previous Balance:

Ending Balance:

Transaction Date	Description	Debit (withdrawals)	Credit (Deposits)	Balance
Total Transactions				

MONTHLY BANK RECONCILIATION STATEMENT

SUMMARY

Period:

Previous Balance:

Ending Balance:

Transaction Date	Description	Debit (withdrawals)	Credit (Deposits)	Balance
Total Transactions				

MONTHLY BANK RECONCILIATION STATEMENT

SUMMARY

Period:

Previous Balance:

Ending Balance:

Transaction Date	Description	Debit (withdrawals)	Credit (Deposits)	Balance
Total Transactions				

MONTHLY BANK RECONCILIATION STATEMENT

SUMMARY

Period:

Previous Balance:

Ending Balance:

Transaction Date	Description	Debit (withdrawals)	Credit (Deposits)	Balance
Total Transactions				

MONTHLY BANK RECONCILIATION STATEMENT

SUMMARY

Period:

Previous Balance:

Ending Balance:

Transaction Date	Description	Debit (withdrawals)	Credit (Deposits)	Balance
Total Transactions				

MONTHLY BANK RECONCILIATION STATEMENT

SUMMARY

Period:

Previous Balance:

Ending Balance:

Transaction Date	Description	Debit (withdrawals)	Credit (Deposits)	Balance
Total Transactions				

MONTHLY BANK RECONCILIATION STATEMENT

SUMMARY

Period:

Previous Balance:

Ending Balance:

Transaction Date	Description	Debit (withdrawals)	Credit (Deposits)	Balance
Total Transactions				

MONTHLY BANK RECONCILIATION STATEMENT

SUMMARY

Period:

Previous Balance:

Ending Balance:

Transaction Date	Description	Debit (withdrawals)	Credit (Deposits)	Balance
Total Transactions				

MONTHLY BANK RECONCILIATION STATEMENT

SUMMARY

Period:

Previous Balance:

Ending Balance:

Transaction Date	Description	Debit (withdrawals)	Credit (Deposits)	Balance
Total Transactions				

MONTHLY BANK RECONCILIATION STATEMENT

SUMMARY

Period:

Previous Balance:

Ending Balance:

Transaction Date	Description	Debit (withdrawals)	Credit (Deposits)	Balance
Total Transactions				

MONTHLY BANK RECONCILIATION STATEMENT

SUMMARY

Period:

Previous Balance:

Ending Balance:

Transaction Date	Description	Debit (withdrawals)	Credit (Deposits)	Balance
Total Transactions				

MONTHLY BANK RECONCILIATION STATEMENT

SUMMARY

Period:

Previous Balance:

Ending Balance:

Transaction Date	Description	Debit (withdrawals)	Credit (Deposits)	Balance
Total Transactions				

MONTHLY BANK RECONCILIATION STATEMENT

SUMMARY

Period:

Previous Balance:

Ending Balance:

Transaction Date	Description	Debit (withdrawals)	Credit (Deposits)	Balance
Total Transactions				

MONTHLY BANK RECONCILIATION STATEMENT

SUMMARY

Period:

Previous Balance:

Ending Balance:

Transaction Date	Description	Debit (withdrawals)	Credit (Deposits)	Balance
Total Transactions				

MONTHLY BANK RECONCILIATION STATEMENT

SUMMARY

Period:

Previous Balance:

Ending Balance:

Transaction Date	Description	Debit (withdrawals)	Credit (Deposits)	Balance
Total Transactions				

MONTHLY BANK RECONCILIATION STATEMENT

SUMMARY

Period:

Previous Balance:

Ending Balance:

Transaction Date	Description	Debit (withdrawals)	Credit (Deposits)	Balance
Total Transactions				

MONTHLY BANK RECONCILIATION STATEMENT

SUMMARY

Period:

Previous Balance:

Ending Balance:

Transaction Date	Description	Debit (withdrawals)	Credit (Deposits)	Balance
Total Transactions				

MONTHLY BANK RECONCILIATION STATEMENT

SUMMARY

Period:

Previous Balance:

Ending Balance:

Transaction Date	Description	Debit (withdrawals)	Credit (Deposits)	Balance
Total Transactions				

MONTHLY BANK RECONCILIATION STATEMENT

SUMMARY

Period:

Previous Balance:

Ending Balance:

Transaction Date	Description	Debit (withdrawals)	Credit (Deposits)	Balance
Total Transactions				

MONTHLY BANK RECONCILIATION STATEMENT

SUMMARY

Period:

Previous Balance:

Ending Balance:

Transaction Date	Description	Debit (withdrawals)	Credit (Deposits)	Balance
Total Transactions				

MONTHLY BANK RECONCILIATION STATEMENT

SUMMARY

Period:

Previous Balance:

Ending Balance:

Transaction Date	Description	Debit (withdrawals)	Credit (Deposits)	Balance
Total Transactions				

MONTHLY BANK RECONCILIATION STATEMENT

SUMMARY

Period:

Previous Balance:

Ending Balance:

Transaction Date	Description	Debit (withdrawals)	Credit (Deposits)	Balance
Total Transactions				

MONTHLY BANK RECONCILIATION STATEMENT

SUMMARY

Period:

Previous Balance:

Ending Balance:

Transaction Date	Description	Debit (withdrawals)	Credit (Deposits)	Balance
Total Transactions				

MONTHLY BANK RECONCILIATION STATEMENT

SUMMARY

Period:

Previous Balance:

Ending Balance:

Transaction Date	Description	Debit (withdrawals)	Credit (Deposits)	Balance
Total Transactions				

MONTHLY BANK RECONCILIATION STATEMENT

SUMMARY

Period:

Previous Balance:

Ending Balance:

Transaction Date	Description	Debit (withdrawals)	Credit (Deposits)	Balance
Total Transactions				

MONTHLY BANK RECONCILIATION STATEMENT

SUMMARY

Period:

Previous Balance:

Ending Balance:

Transaction Date	Description	Debit (withdrawals)	Credit (Deposits)	Balance
Total Transactions				

MONTHLY BANK RECONCILIATION STATEMENT

SUMMARY

Period:

Previous Balance:

Ending Balance:

Transaction Date	Description	Debit (withdrawals)	Credit (Deposits)	Balance
Total Transactions				

MONTHLY BANK RECONCILIATION STATEMENT

SUMMARY

Period:

Previous Balance:

Ending Balance:

Transaction Date	Description	Debit (withdrawals)	Credit (Deposits)	Balance
Total Transactions				

MONTHLY BANK RECONCILIATION STATEMENT

SUMMARY

Period:

Previous Balance:

Ending Balance:

Transaction Date	Description	Debit (withdrawals)	Credit (Deposits)	Balance
Total Transactions				

MONTHLY BANK RECONCILIATION STATEMENT

SUMMARY

Period:

Previous Balance:

Ending Balance:

Transaction Date	Description	Debit (withdrawals)	Credit (Deposits)	Balance
Total Transactions				

MONTHLY BANK RECONCILIATION STATEMENT

SUMMARY

Period:

Previous Balance:

Ending Balance:

Transaction Date	Description	Debit (withdrawals)	Credit (Deposits)	Balance
Total Transactions				

MONTHLY BANK RECONCILIATION STATEMENT

SUMMARY

Period:

Previous Balance:

Ending Balance:

Transaction Date	Description	Debit (withdrawals)	Credit (Deposits)	Balance
Total Transactions				

MONTHLY BANK RECONCILIATION STATEMENT

SUMMARY

Period:

Previous Balance:

Ending Balance:

Transaction Date	Description	Debit (withdrawals)	Credit (Deposits)	Balance
Total Transactions				

MONTHLY BANK RECONCILIATION STATEMENT

SUMMARY

Period:

Previous Balance:

Ending Balance:

Transaction Date	Description	Debit (withdrawals)	Credit (Deposits)	Balance
Total Transactions				

MONTHLY BANK RECONCILIATION STATEMENT

SUMMARY

Period:

Previous Balance:

Ending Balance:

Transaction Date	Description	Debit (withdrawals)	Credit (Deposits)	Balance
Total Transactions				

MONTHLY BANK RECONCILIATION STATEMENT

SUMMARY

Period:

Previous Balance:

Ending Balance:

Transaction Date	Description	Debit (withdrawals)	Credit (Deposits)	Balance
Total Transactions				

MONTHLY BANK RECONCILIATION STATEMENT

SUMMARY

Period:

Previous Balance:

Ending Balance:

Transaction Date	Description	Debit (withdrawals)	Credit (Deposits)	Balance
Total Transactions				

MONTHLY BANK RECONCILIATION STATEMENT

SUMMARY

Period:

Previous Balance:

Ending Balance:

Transaction Date	Description	Debit (withdrawals)	Credit (Deposits)	Balance
Total Transactions				

MONTHLY BANK RECONCILIATION STATEMENT

SUMMARY

Period:

Previous Balance:

Ending Balance:

Transaction Date	Description	Debit (withdrawals)	Credit (Deposits)	Balance
Total Transactions				

MONTHLY BANK RECONCILIATION STATEMENT

SUMMARY

Period:

Previous Balance:

Ending Balance:

Transaction Date	Description	Debit (withdrawals)	Credit (Deposits)	Balance
Total Transactions				

MONTHLY BANK RECONCILIATION STATEMENT

SUMMARY

Period:

Previous Balance:

Ending Balance:

Transaction Date	Description	Debit (withdrawals)	Credit (Deposits)	Balance
Total Transactions				

MONTHLY BANK RECONCILIATION STATEMENT

SUMMARY

Period:

Previous Balance:

Ending Balance:

Transaction Date	Description	Debit (withdrawals)	Credit (Deposits)	Balance
Total Transactions				

MONTHLY BANK RECONCILIATION STATEMENT

SUMMARY

Period:

Previous Balance:

Ending Balance:

Transaction Date	Description	Debit (withdrawals)	Credit (Deposits)	Balance
Total Transactions				

MONTHLY BANK RECONCILIATION STATEMENT

SUMMARY

Period:

Previous Balance:

Ending Balance:

Transaction Date	Description	Debit (withdrawals)	Credit (Deposits)	Balance
Total Transactions				

MONTHLY BANK RECONCILIATION STATEMENT

SUMMARY

Period:

Previous Balance:

Ending Balance:

Transaction Date	Description	Debit (withdrawals)	Credit (Deposits)	Balance
Total Transactions				

MONTHLY BANK RECONCILIATION STATEMENT

SUMMARY

Period:

Previous Balance:

Ending Balance:

Transaction Date	Description	Debit (withdrawals)	Credit (Deposits)	Balance
Total Transactions				

MONTHLY BANK RECONCILIATION STATEMENT

SUMMARY

Period:

Previous Balance:

Ending Balance:

Transaction Date	Description	Debit (withdrawals)	Credit (Deposits)	Balance
Total Transactions				

MONTHLY BANK RECONCILIATION STATEMENT

SUMMARY

Period:

Previous Balance:

Ending Balance:

Transaction Date	Description	Debit (withdrawals)	Credit (Deposits)	Balance
Total Transactions				

MONTHLY BANK RECONCILIATION STATEMENT

SUMMARY

Period:

Previous Balance:

Ending Balance:

Transaction Date	Description	Debit (withdrawals)	Credit (Deposits)	Balance
Total Transactions				

MONTHLY BANK RECONCILIATION STATEMENT

SUMMARY

Period:

Previous Balance:

Ending Balance:

Transaction Date	Description	Debit (withdrawals)	Credit (Deposits)	Balance
Total Transactions				

MONTHLY BANK RECONCILIATION STATEMENT

SUMMARY

Period:

Previous Balance:

Ending Balance:

Transaction Date	Description	Debit (withdrawals)	Credit (Deposits)	Balance
Total Transactions				

MONTHLY BANK RECONCILIATION STATEMENT

SUMMARY

Period:

Previous Balance:

Ending Balance:

Transaction Date	Description	Debit (withdrawals)	Credit (Deposits)	Balance
Total Transactions				

MONTHLY BANK RECONCILIATION STATEMENT

SUMMARY

Period:

Previous Balance:

Ending Balance:

Transaction Date	Description	Debit (withdrawals)	Credit (Deposits)	Balance
Total Transactions				

MONTHLY BANK RECONCILIATION STATEMENT

SUMMARY

Period:

Previous Balance:

Ending Balance:

Transaction Date	Description	Debit (withdrawals)	Credit (Deposits)	Balance
Total Transactions				

MONTHLY BANK RECONCILIATION STATEMENT

SUMMARY

Period:

Previous Balance:

Ending Balance:

Transaction Date	Description	Debit (withdrawals)	Credit (Deposits)	Balance
Total Transactions				

MONTHLY BANK RECONCILIATION STATEMENT

SUMMARY

Period:

Previous Balance:

Ending Balance:

Transaction Date	Description	Debit (withdrawals)	Credit (Deposits)	Balance
Total Transactions				

MONTHLY BANK RECONCILIATION STATEMENT

		SUMMARY		
Period:				
Previous Balance:				
Ending Balance:				
Transaction Date	**Description**	**Debit (withdrawals)**	**Credit (Deposits)**	**Balance**
Total Transactions				

www.ingramcontent.com/pod-product-compliance
Lightning Source LLC
Chambersburg PA
CBHW081202180526
45170CB00006B/2187
9781546505730